A

Small

Revolt

Poetry from within ~ without

Yasmeen Hamzeh

inner child press, ltd.

Credits

Author
Yasmeen Hamzeh

Foreword
Nizar Sartawi

Editor
hülya n. yılmaz, Ph.D.

Cover Design
Inner Child Press, ltd.

Editor's Note

As the Director of the Editing Department for Inner Child Press International, I must express my utter delight in working on the manuscript of Yasmeen Hamzeh, a native speaker of Arabic. Contextual challenges often reside in the writings of non-native English speakers or in works translated into English. This poetic compilation by Ms. Hamzeh rises far above the norm in its entirety.

hülya n. yılmaz, Ph.D.
Director of Editing
Emerita, Penn State University

General Information

A Small Revolt
Author: Yasmeen Hamzeh

1st Edition: 2019

Publisher Information
1st Edition: Inner Child Press
intouch@innerchildpress.com
www.innerchildpress.com

ISBN-13: 978-1-970020-98-4 (inner child press, ltd.)

$ 12.99

Dedication

This poetry collection is dedicated to my biggest support and inspiration – my father R.H., and to my eternal muse – life.

Table of Contents

The Poetry

Table of Contents . . . *continued*

Introduction

A Small Revolt holds in its pages intricate poems that dazzle the reader with a delicate language. This collection is the first work of a gifted young woman who expresses her feelings in honest images, with her own beauty illuminating her writing.

Yasmeen Hamzeeh writes poetry in words that radiate warmth and intimacy, embossed with letters in the light of candles when the night languishes in her enticing style, engrained with beautiful prose and a deep understanding of all that is happening around her on the paths of life.

This book announces the birth of a poet, and she will have in the future other collections of poems which will delight the hearts of her readers.

Samih Massoud
Poet and writer

Preface

This poetry collection is my first venture into publishing. It gives me great joy to be able to share all these personal and hopefully enlightening pieces of myself. I am a yet-to-be established writer, still finding my footing. During my current journey into finishing my first degree, my writings have become an anchor to which I can hang onto during any turbulence I encountered along the way. I have been writing as far back as I can remember and slowly trying to create my own identity as a writer.

I started confiding in poetry while I was still in middle school, and found it to be a comfortable outlet. It used to fill the long silences which I was assigned with at that tender age. There was so much raging within me that I could not explain or understand. I felt the need to explore myself and delve in deeper, but I needed a judgement-free environment in which I could do that safely. Not only did writing help, but it also created a shield when things got rough.

I experienced many challenges during my high-school years. I had to overcome numerous personal issues that began to take over my life. When it came to writing, I could express what I felt and give voice to my thoughts and ideas. It slowly helped me regain my confidence in the darkest of times, and helped me create a persona strong enough to handle a reality that seemed adamant on tearing me down. I carried on writing throughout high school, while also being published in yearly school magazines.

Being born as a Middle Eastern woman has always come with its challenges. My varying experiences as a person who had struggled with creating an identity in the midst of a difficult society taught me a lot about the world around me. Living in such a contradictory culture that seemed to clash with the advancements of our world made it difficult for me to set a specific moral compass, and thus, it took a lot of searching and self-discovery to be able to deal with such a feat. These experiences have shaped my writings at large and the poems that I present in this collection. It is a representation of a journey, or an odyssey – a road I walked on towards an understanding of myself, the world around me and the way I felt about both.

As a child, the biggest influence in my life was my father. My mother had passed away when I was still very young, and so my father took on the role of both parent figures, which strengthened my bond with him as a father, confidant and friend. He has always been a person that valued knowledge and understanding, thus he always encouraged me to go out into the world with curious eyes. He taught me the importance of books and their effect on a person. His interest in books helped him achieve a unique outlook and creed in life, all shaped by his hunger for unbiased knowledge. The older I grew the more infatuated I became with my father's view of life. He was my idol and I truly aspired to become like him, a unique individual with all the strength knowledge could grant you. So, I began to read, and my interpretations of this knowledge began to flow through my pen.

It was my own take on life, my own warping of knowledge and experience that soon materialized. As a native Arabic speaker, I decided to branch out and focused on grasping an understanding of the English language. This dedication fueled me to start writing in English so that I may expand my knowledge and skills. A combination of my interest in different styles of poetry, varying from sonnets to post-modern prose has also given me the tools to create my own stylistic experience as a writer. I am presenting in this collection an experience, or a glimpse into my psyche. I hope it takes you on this journey which details my sorrows, confusion, heartbreaks, and strength amongst other emotions I had faced. I am baring my soul, and it makes me nervous but also delighted to be able to share my knowledge and opinions.

Foreword

A Small Revolt by Yasmeen Hamzeh: A Vision Quest

After a long journey
I have found you.

Now resting at your threshold
in this moonlit night,

I'm waiting for you to know
that I'm here.

I have come all the way
not to try your love for me;

I'm here to tell –
I can't afford not to love anymore!

Kalpna Singh Chitnis ("Ancient Quest II", *Bare Soul*)

Yasmeen Hamzeh is a new female Jordanian poetic voice, who, unlike the majority of her fellow Jordanian poets, writes in English. Making her debut with this poetry collection, *A Small Revolt*, while still working on her first college degree, Yasmeen has forged for herself a new path at an early stage in her life – a path that could evolve into a full literary career if the young poet is inclined to pursue such a path.

The title of Yasmeen's poetry book is rather curious. It recalls literary groups, such as the beat generation – the post-war poets whose movement emerged in the USA and flourished in 1950s and 60's, revolting against the values and traditions of the earlier generation. Interestingly, like the beat poets, Yasmeen belongs to a new generation, or age group, arising in the Middle East amidst the conflicts, upheavals and tribulations that have swept through the region in the last seven or eight years. *A Small Revolt*, however, is shorn of the political and social implications of these unfortunate events.

Revolt can be viewed as the common thread that binds the poems in this collection. It must be remembered, though, that revolt often happens as a result of discontent with or resentment of a status quo, and therefore it aims at effecting change. Also, like its other synonyms – riot, rebellion, mutiny, etc. – revolt is usually associated with violence. The poet, however, mitigates this quality by describing it as "small," probably because it is a quiet, noiseless type of "revolt" that tends to be personal in nature. It is mainly occurring within the poet herself, or rather within the persona in her poetry, often taking the form of an internal monologue, or inner speech, through which the reader is allowed to have a glimpse of her persona, but it also serves to build her self-awareness and change her outlook or behavior as a result of the learning process she goes through.

In this sense, *A Small Revolt* is about a spiritual journey, in which the persona keeps examining and re-examining her thoughts, feelings, and inner conflicts. Significantly, the poet mentions this journey in the very first poem, "My Quilt of Reality", where she speaks of "My own bible / dictating the journey."

The journey begins in the first poem and continues throughout the book, but the metaphors for it keep shifting. In the very first poem, for instance, the poet uses four words contextually associated with journeying – wind, flight and road:

[. . .]
and there's no wind to carry me asunder,
[. . .]
the reason for my continuing fight.
[. . .]
A road marred by filth,
[. . .]

In other poems, the road is used in different contexts and images. "The Thrill" speaks of "a road on your skin," something like the lines on one's palm that chorologists or fortune tellers can read and interpret. In "A Road, Revisited", the title word is repeated in three lines:

[. . .]
but a road will be waiting.
[. . .]
[P]ushing away that road you fear.
[. . .]
That road wraps around your eyes,
[. . .]

The road also recurs in other poems, including "The Endless U-Turn", "Peaks, Never Reached", "An Obsession", and "A Final Comfort in Loss". Likewise, the word "path," a synonym of road, is repeated in "An Obsession", where the poet describes the divergence between her heart and mind with regard to her journey: "My heart beats on a path / my mind can't control."

Other, more sophisticated metaphors of the journey include spatial references, such as the sea and expanses. Thus, in "Longing", the poet becomes a mariner, whose sea "wraps [her] up / in a cold breeze / that whispers defeat". In "Peaks, Never Reached", she finds herself "[b]etween all those dark roads / and empty expanses".

In many respects, the poet's journey is an initiation ritual – one that resembles the trip, commonly known as a "vision quest," usually undertaken by aboriginal people in many parts of the world. For example, the Nez Perce tribe, an indigenous people who have lived for a long time in the Pacific Northwest lands of the USA, would send their young males on an initiation trip just before they reach adulthood. Guided by elders of the community, each young man would go by himself across hills and mountains, stepping on thorns and sharp stones. He would spend days and nights walking, fasting, praying, and calling the spirits in the hope of having a dream or vision. Later, he would ask the elders to interpret his vision, which usually serves as guidance for him to find meaning or purpose in life and learn ways to help the people of his tribe.

In Yasmeen's poems, the persona's journey does have some commonalities with the vision quest: For example, her "own bible" ("My Quilt of Reality") plays the role of the elders, indicating that embarking on a journey is a creed, an inevitable action that is enforced by a powerful doctrine. The obstacles lying in her path, such as the "dampened plateaus," "dark roads," and "empty expanses" ("Peaks, Never Reached") parallel the hardships encountered by the vision questers. Her physical suffering, as depicted in "Awakening", for

instance, resembles the pains and agonies experienced
by the young tribesmen:

> Numb extremities
> can't hold much at bay.
> I've lost my arm's strength,
> [. . .]
> just as I was walking
> blind and scared.
> Now, each step
> makes me want to
> regurgitate,
> [. . .]
> and I now can see all the blood
> staining my skin,
> see it all seeping into my pores.

Likewise, the dreams and visions that the young people
have during their trip are also experienced by the poet.
Dreaming is apparently one of the major motifs in
Yasmeen's poems. The word "dream" itself appears
multiple times in the book; twice, as daydreams. Two
others are used in poem titles: "Of Distant Dreams" and
"A Dream, Not a Promise". At the beginning, dreams
are a source of fear and anxiety, as the following lines
from "Of Distant Dreams" show:

> My dreams have become
> frighteningly beautiful,
> a painful lucidity,
> a cry for anything,
> except for this shadowing angst.

In "The Endless U-Turn", the visions seem to suggest
that the persona is torn from inside: "Visions of clashing
/ and wreckage, / a dream of laying everything / to
waste." But they also point to physical pains she suffers,

surprisingly similar to those which Perce Nez vision questers are exposed to: "I'm treading on broken glass, / hoping my feet recognize the pain."

This resemblance that the poet's journey bears with the tribal vision quest is of course symbolic rather than actual. The vision quest, which is a rite of passage, is undertaken physically by the individual, who goes on an actual trip in order to prove that he is qualified to move to another age group. The poet's odyssey, on the other hand, takes place in a different dimension: the poet's own world – her mind or psyche. We, the readers, know about it only through her poetry. Moreover, taking a journey on the poet's part is a personal choice. It is neither ordained by the community, nor undertaken by her age group. In fact, it sets her apart from her generation, as she asserts in her poem, "Of Distant Dreams":

> Kids my age are running around,
> pretending to fall in love;
> letting their pent-up rage explode;
> getting their hearts broken,
> and struggling
> with their achievements.
> [. . .]
> Kids my age are waiting
> for that phone to finally ring;
> waiting for admiration
> to be bestowed upon them
> for their faces to be recognized.
> While I lack conviction.

For her, the thoughts and acts of the "kids my age" are quite superficial. These kids occupy themselves with pretenses, insignificant accomplishments, and false feelings – the immature comforts of young people. She, on the other hand, is immersed in deep thoughts, trying to disentangle herself from these juvenile engagements. She has a far more serious mission, which is to come to grips with the more profound meaning of life, to connect it with a purpose:

> While I sit around and play pretend,
> dramatizing what love would feel like;
> wishing to be broken
> just to feel the pain;
> hoping that one day
> I can write down my own destiny;
> swearing that the next time
> wouldn't be the same,
> that I would make someone proud.
> [. . .]
> My mind has taken my body captive,
> entangling it with strings of delusion.
> A life so empty
> you compress it
> into a digitalized document,
> only consisting of pages
> filled with unfinished stories.

Apparently, the poet's journey is largely driven by her frustration with and fear of the realities of this world, in which she feels alienated. This phenomenon is reflected in numerous images, such as the "fragile balance" and "chills of danger" ("The Thrill"), "swinging bats and / heavy chains" ("A Confession"), "waves of sand", ("A Road, Revisited'), "[a] sea of contradictions" ("Anxiety Fears Company"), "[v]isions of clashing and wreckage" ("The Endless U-Turn"), the 'horrifying coldness' ("Limerence"), "plastic roses" ("An Obsession"), and "[s]oaked sponges suffocating / and filling the void. / Cowering in disgust" ("The Collateral").

These negative feelings are further echoed in her physical, mental, and emotional state. "[P]iece by piece I am torn apart", says the poet in "My Quilt of Reality":

> A piece for the misled,
> a piece for the cornered,
> and a piece for the whirlwind.
> Now, I am a preserved bone,
> doused in firewater.
> Gnashing teeth,
> all too familiar.
> Ache of muscles,
> too safe.

Depictions like this are found in almost every poem, where the poet examines, analyzes, and describes the details of the body, mind and psyche of her persona. It is interesting to note how the poet often handles her persona as though she were a patient being treated by a physician or psychiatrist, and to observe how the voice changes from one poem to another according to the speaker's role. In "A Road, Revisited", for instance, the speaker assumes the rule of a physician talking about, rather than to, their patient by using the third person in describing the symptoms of weakness that takes a hold of her:

> She has fizzled out.
> Once a bright young swallow.
> Dark irises that once held
> a shred of talent
> have lost their luster.

The picture, however, is not totally objective, or impersonal. The reference to "Once a bright young swallow" and the "shred of talent" once held by "[d]ark irises" are far from being clinical. They register a sympathetic, compassionate tone on the part of the poet, revealing her affinity with the persona.

In "The Thrill", the persona – now the patient – is in a state of confusion, uncertainty, and irresolution, as the perplexed questions in her internal monologue suggest:

> What if that fragile balance fractures?
> Which side would you choose?
> Would you handle going
> against yourself,
> against the very vibrations
> passing through your body?
> Or would you risk shredding
> what little peace of mind is left?
> The cold metallic feel brushes
> against your hands.
> Do you pull the trigger?

In other poems, the monologue turns into a series of recommendations expressed in the imperative. "A Confession", for instance, which consists of 47 lines, contains 25 verbal commands, including the following:

> Season yourself in distrust,
> and soak in bleach.
> Learn to draw
> the perfect blood-red lip,
> and adjust to the grip of lace strings,
> [. . .]
> Saunter to the beat of flowing drinks,
> [. . .]

Let the strength of suggestion
take over,
[. . .]
Crave the rattling call of forgetfulness,
sit between walls,
wondering if time is a balm.

Similar commands are used in "A Road, Revisited":

Get back down
and feast your eyes
on this locked chest.
Open it and find nothing,
[. . .]
Get back down
and feast your eyes
on an old man,
waiting for the chance to smile.
[. . .]
Watch as waves of sand
wash over the possibilities
of that smile.
Watch as each string snaps,
bleeding away years.

Evidently, such commands serve collectively as a defense mechanism to which the poet resorts in her resolution to keep a stiff upper lip, thus refraining from showing or feeling emotions. In this sense, she is like Sisyphus, the Corinthian king, who was condemned to roll a heavy boulder up a hill, only to see it fall again just before it reached the top.

So, where does this journey or vision quest eventually lead to? Does it end where it has begun, as is suggested in some poems? Does the persona "Tip-toe [her] way /

back into the emptiness" ("A Road, Revisited"), or is it thus that "[s]omething [she] saw / pulls [her] back" ("An Observation")?

Obviously, the poet, or persona, is able to accomplish her mission successfully. Despite the disappointments, losses and failures, she finally comes out whole, more powerful and resolute than ever before, as the last several poems in the collection indicate. In "Growth", for instance, the tone shifts completely from uncertainty to confidence:

> You take your steps
>   with confidence,
>   your hips sway
>   and a familiar smile
>   paints your lips.

She has come to grips with the balanced equation of life, accommodating both successes and failures. She learns how to overcome her frailty, how to cope with her weaknesses, how to rise again when she falls or fails:

[. . .]

> Strength shines through
>   and shrouds your yearnings
>   and weaknesses.
> The pillar you represent
>   is a sword to fight off loss
>   and hurt.
>   You are light,
>   intertwined with my darkness.
>   The swirling fear dissipates
>   with each word you say,
>   like a prayer.

You stand and fall,
but you always fight.

The idea of balancing gain and loss is developed further in the poem titled "Strength", in which she emphasizes that she has not lost hope:

Feet rooted
  deep in the ground,
    head held up high.
      Tides wash over.
       The moon
         illuminates the loss,
           but remains unwavering.

The cycle of struggle
  is never-ending.

Hope is born
  out of revelations.
    Hope tells me,
      I'm still existent,
       still alive,
         and I can make it through.

The poem ends with two lines, asserting that she will continue her journey. Like the famed Japanese mountaineer who reached the top of Mount Fuji hundreds of times, and is now saying he is ready for Everest, Yasmeen Hamzeh is ready to carry on, to explore higher horizons. "My knees haven't weakened," she proclaims, "and I still have miles to soar."

Reaching the peak, her whole outlook changes dramatically in "Epiphany":

Appreciate it,
but do you observe the harmony

as a whole?
I see life in color,
not in black and white.

The last two poems, "Despite Your Malignances" and
"A Final Comfort in Loss", serving as a denouement to
her pilgrimage and the preparation for a new adventure,
are reserved for self-reassurance and determination. In
the former, she asserts herself as a strong being, who has
not only gained self-knowledge, but who is also aware
of her milieu and the dangers that may lie ahead. But
she is far from being timid or hesitant, to which the
poet's own words attest in the latter:

[. . .]

Standing fully erect,
        fully aware of the surroundings.
            Ahead lay a dark and gaping forest.
            A sudden twitch,
                signaling the overcoming shivering.
                Deeper into the forest,
                    lulled by a strange force.

Trudging through untamed wilderness.
    Feet never faltering,
[. . .]

In "Despite Your Malignances", getting ready to
embark on her new odyssey, she assures herself again:

You can sail the world
in your plight,
and take a look around.
Here I am,
standing at a crossroad.

> My tresses,
> blowing left and right.

At this point, she experiences yet another growth spurt; she feels that she has become part of nature when a tree comes into view in the same poem, and new thoughts pass through her mind:

> A long and ever-gazing tree,
> wise with the past
> and words of those who
> passed.
> The trunk may be sturdy,
> but the roots take a hold
> in old soil.
> The howling wind sends it shuddering,
> but my feet have learned to
> dance along to the tune.

It is rather surprising, how this affinity with the wind co-incidentally bears remarkable resemblance with one of the basic tenets of the vision quest undertaken by the young men of Nez Perce mentioned earlier; namely, the connection with nature.

Have these poems been written by the poet just for the poet? Perhaps not. Somehow, we might feel that they have been written for us too. Perhaps we all have this potential of becoming one with nature, singing its songs through poetry or another form of art. But to do so, we may have to take our own spiritual pilgrimage to undertake the vision quest, so to speak. Life then may gift us with the power to shape our destiny as Yasmeen Hamzeh, who sings towards the end of "Despite Your Malignancies:

Like clay, I shape my psyche,
molding my own version of reality.
Like holding on
to a rocking boat
where each stalemate
tries to topple me over.

Nizar Sartawi
Poet and Translator

A

Small

Revolt

Poetry from within ~ without

Yasmeen Hamzeh

The Poetry

Yasmeen Hamzeh

My Quilt of Reality

A sliver of skin,
piece by piece I am torn apart.
A piece for the misled,
a piece for the cornered,
and a piece for the whirlwind.
Now, I am a preserved bone,
doused in firewater.
Gnashing teeth,
all too familiar.
Ache of muscles,
too safe.
Run towards grief,
like a cloak to be burrowed under.
When it gets too warm
and there's no wind to carry me asunder,
beg for relief of a tedious space.
A withstanding archive of strife.
A record of mistakes and unspoken truths.
My own bible,
dictating the journey.
The reason for holding on,
the reason for my continuing fight.
A doctrine of loss, battle, and surrender.
A road marred by filth,
with landscapes of beauty,
but most of all blessed with honesty.
A scream for all the ones
willing to withstand the pain.
The ones who revel
in each raw bruise,

Yasmeen Hamzeh

watching colors reflect
the movement of time.
To be unleashed,
not by existing shackles
but the ones melded by my mind.
Not a day in the sun,
but a comfort in the darkness as it descends.

The Thrill

Draw the line.
Keep telling yourself
you know where your feet tread.
What if that fragile balance fractures?
Which side would you choose?
Would you handle going
against yourself,
against the very vibrations
passing through your body?
Or would you risk shredding
what little peace of mind is left?
The cold metallic feel brushes
against your hands.
Do you pull the trigger?
I can't contain the possibilities,
especially when I reminisce.
At night, I ran,
barely dodging scattered wooden chairs.
An echo of temptation
beckoned me further.
How thrilling to live
between the creases of each lie!
How perfect
to let the chills of danger
spread a road on your skin,
to let words touch lips
as they splatter out
and run with the wind!
An affair
with the more plausible mistake.

Yasmeen Hamzeh

You reek of danger,
but my heart found a home in fear,
and so, you must
taste sweet.
I want to hurt, shred and slash.
I want to rule my kingdom on pillars of empathy and
psychosis.

A Confession

Learn to feign ignorance,
let the knife sink deeper.
Learn to sniff the dirt
in their nails.
Switch cards
and always keep one
under your sleeve.
Slit your tongue in half
and spin words,
learn to discard the weak.
Taste the succulent bitterness,
teach your head
to deal with the pressure.
Suddenly, develop an addiction
to the rush of blood
and the hidden compartments
between folds of skin.
Find yourself lacing
your running shoes,
a race away from liability.
Learn the sound of
crunching bones,
and study the shape of fading bruises.
It gets easy to learn the smell
of interchanging sheets,
even while dodging swinging bats
and heavy chains.
Season yourself in distrust,
and soak in bleach.
Learn to draw

the perfect blood-red lip,
and adjust to the grip of lace strings,
adding more to a ledger already overflowing.
Saunter to the beat of flowing drinks,
while ignoring dirt
under your own nails.
Let the strength of suggestion
take over,
because it's easy to lose to the battle of time.
Crave the rattling call of forgetfulness,
sit between walls,
wondering if time is a balm.
Hope for the oversight of purity
and the grip of control over filth.
Questions and methods are in abundance.
So, seek martyrdom
in the name of an answer.

A Road, Revisited

She has fizzled out.
Once a bright young swallow.
Dark irises that once held
a shred of talent
have lost their luster.
When will you give up
on this paper version of a thrill?
Get back down
and feast your eyes
on this locked chest.
Open it and find nothing,
but a road will be waiting.
It only promises
to turn you hardened and empty,
cutting the last strings
tied to you.
Get back down
and feast your eyes
on an old man,
waiting for the chance to smile.
His lamenting fingers balled up,
pushing away that road you fear.
No use in remembering
each stalemate.
Tip-toe your way
back into the emptiness.
It will hold you in its arms
and keep you safe.
Watch as waves of sand
wash over the possibilities

of that smile.
Watch as each string snaps,
bleeding away years.
That road wraps around your eyes,
effectively rendering you sightless.
She shall hold the trifling prize,
willing to feast her eyes
on that man swelling with pride.
Empty and hollow,
but comforted by that smile.
A smile her kaleidoscope
had once drowned.

Of Distant Dreams

Kids my age are running around,
pretending to fall in love;
letting their pent-up rage explode;
getting their hearts broken,
and struggling
with their achievements.
While I sit around and play pretend,
dramatizing what love would feel like;
wishing to be broken
just to feel the pain;
hoping that one day
I can write down my own destiny;
swearing that the next time
wouldn't be the same,
that I would make someone proud.
It's hard forgetting how to live.
All that's left are fragments.
Always running away
towards guilt,
strung between the wish to be numb
and suspension of time,
I find myself
belonging to contradiction.
I wish for pain
but fear it.
I wish for closure
but run from it.
I hope for success
but my feet carry me farther away.
My dreams have become

frighteningly beautiful,
a painful lucidity,
a cry for anything,
except for this shadowing angst.
Kids my age are waiting
for that phone to finally ring;
waiting for admiration
to be bestowed upon them
for their faces to be recognized,
while I lack conviction.
My mind has taken my body captive,
entangling it with strings of delusion.
A life so empty
you compress it
into a digitalized document,
only consisting of pages
filled with unfinished stories.

An Observation

You observe.
I know what you see.
It's all perfectly visual.
Your eyes low to the ground,
they catch on the tip of her heel.
You follow the curve of the red sole
to reach her thin ankle.
Something possesses you
to look further up,
and unintentionally trace the
expanse of her languid legs.
Suddenly, her eyes are staring
back at you,
and all you can do
is instantly turn away.
Something you saw
pulls you back, and you look.
Her lips are red,
darker than blood,
and her eyes remain in your direction.
She removes the cigarette
from her lips,
and the look in her eyes
almost throws
you off your chair.
You train your eyes
to look straight ahead,
but when you close your eyes,
an image flashes.
An image of her lips

pressed against the concrete.
Your eyes open
only to redirect towards her.
Her black rimmed eyes
with irises that seem desolate
are redirected away from you.
When you close your eyes,
another image flashes . . .
An image of her dead eyes
staring up at you,
almost pleading.

A Struggle

I watch as eyes
turn a reddish hue.
It doesn't change a thing,
feels like a vacuum.
I detest this self,
this existing mistake.
A fear of this nonexistent reflection,
knowing on the inside
what I will find.
I feel like clenching my heart
within my own fist
just to remember
that once persistent beating.
Reaching towards my ribcage,
it only meets rotten flesh.
It seems like time
has run away from me,
but it's the same ceiling
I stare at.
Words spoken
with no meaning,
no emotion . . .
Reality and will
are what we perceive,
and I have lost my sight
for miles.
Opaque, and fragile.
Look closer,
and find stains

marring the silhouette,
stains time can't seem
to wash away.

All that's left
is an attempt to burn them out.

Anxiety Fears Company

Darkness seems to be gnawing
at my skin.
I watch them smile at me
as if I'm ignorant.
They don't know my attempt
at superiority, send me
down the gutter.
So, I sit
picking at my skin,
trying to find strength
between the flakes.
I spread them out and dissect.
A sea of contradictions,
and no one is the wiser.
I feel my convictions melting,
threatening to dissipate
inevitability.
It's my own cruel joke,
playing with control.
Now, I wake up at dusk
screaming,
all the delusions
piling up.
The paws scratching
at the edge of my bed,
the vultures circling the ceiling.
Memories of warm hands,
replaced by cold fingers
at my throat.
I'm instilled

with fear,
a fear of admitting the truth
or reaching for comfort.
Afraid of admitting my wish
for a hand
to hold in the dark.
For I have found horrors
manifesting in hands
faking their warmth.

The Endless U-Turn

The hope is that the sun
shines brighter,
but it just seems
to get dimmer
each time.
I used to believe tugging
at the strings might help.
Instead,
I seem to be drawing nearer
to bleakness,
broken pieces of porcelain,
scattered ashes and slashes
of paint.
Ingredients that stir
in a pot of regret.
My wrists ache
but they long for harsher restraints.
My heart, on the other hand,
is begging for a release.
To the dismay of both,
it seems the coldness
is slowly creeping in.
Nostalgia has become distorted
in its regret.
The hope is that the road
gets clearer.
It just seems to get emptier instead.
Visions of clashing
and wreckage,
a dream of laying everything

to waste,
I'm treading on broken glass,
hoping my feet recognize the pain.
It seems my reflection
has better plans, and I float around instead.

Peaks, Never Reached

The Sun peaks through,
slowly creeps
but finds no solace.
Finding shrouded fears
between darkened sheets . . .
Shrug off
the coat of reality,
and attempt tanning
the long-forgotten skin
for the weeping
that never reaches the eyes,
showered isles
that separate instead.
A reminder
of the dampened plateaus
never reached,
for these hands forgot
how to climb.
Memories fade in and out,
and slip into intertwined arms.
Cauterize those emotions,
the ones that have started to rot.
Between all those dark roads
and empty expanses,
I believe we forgot the feeling.
So, leave me here
to sift between these defeats,
mourning the child
of the blossom.

Growth

It started simple.
  You held on,
    gave me words
      and painted pictures.
        The tip of your tongue
          held words,
            mountains rising
              and rivers running.

The way your eyes dim slowly
  shows the cracks.
    They grow deeper
      and carve their way
        closer to your core.
          Your hidden starlight
            wards away hurt,
              but you don't let it
                seep into you and guide you.

You take your steps
  with confidence,
    your hips sway
      and a familiar smile
        paints your lips.
          Strength shines through
            and shrouds your yearnings
              and weaknesses.

The pillar you represent
is a sword to fight off loss
and hurt.
You are light,
intertwined with my darkness.
The swirling fear dissipates
with each word you say,
like a prayer.

You stand and fall,
but you always fight.

Awakening

This confusion
festers and churns.
Numb extremities
can't hold much at bay.
I've lost my arm's strength,
but my tongue
keeps lashing out.
All these pages
of walking backwards,
yet the vision just gets
unclear and hazy.
The carriage has
found me,
just as I was walking
blind and scared.
Now, each step
makes me want to
regurgitate,
let out all the things
I kept stowing in.
Like daggers
trying to un-cuff me . . .
Not a savior,
but an obsession
to hold me closer . . .
I am the keeper
of these sins,
the caretaker
of these addictions.
But the blindfold slipped,
and I now can see all the blood
staining my skin,
see it all seeping into my pores.

Hung out to Dry

It's supposed to be a fog.
Instead,
it feels like a leash.
Like I'm being tugged,
and immediately
I heed the call.
Soft tendrils
sway me forward
and intoxicate me
with promises of relief.
I find myself lapping
at a river of liquid courage,
blaming my dedication
on a grand mistake –
the tendency to feel only when raw,
confusing,
sickening,
but warm.
My mind has been hanging
sideways,
put out to dry.
It must have been the wind
that carried all this dirt
into the crevices.
Now, I'm left
trying to clean it out,
like picking nettle
from my socks.
It just amounts
to shredded fingertips,

Yasmeen Hamzeh

a ruined pair of socks,
and all this dirt I can't manage
to scrub away.
I'm shedding layers
of sanity and belief.
It seems to be the only retaliation
at losing private pieces of myself.
Now, almost bare to the core,
I search for a coat
to hang on my shoulders.

Limerence

A laughable matter,
how hours seem to change you –
not change you fully,
at least not in the way
a metamorphosis occurs.
It changes the signs of irritation,
the raising alarm,
and mostly adds a deep longing.
A familiar feeling
weighing down each breath.
It feels like a numb explosion;
Like there is more to it,
but it never peaks.
It taunts with promises of relief,
but leaves you boneless.
Instinctively, you mark it
as an unsatisfying end.
You hope for more
and always will.
Maybe it's the stop
of the running clock,
the one that resounds heavily
each night.
The disappointment will dissipate
eventually,
but it feels like centuries
till it does.
The memories keep flashing
like salt;
the familiar sting of shame
from fresh wounds.

The wind you carry with you
drifts you off
to foolish daydreams.
It helps hold back
the inevitable guilt.
Soon, you understand
that this is all erratic;
it must lead to an origin,
one you cannot seem to find.
You realize the attachment to this coldness
is horrifying.
You never plan to become cold;
it just catches fire.
Time takes its toll.
It takes away the chance for amendment,
of retribution.
The obstacles are clearly organized
to hinder a much-needed evolution.

You've Made a Fool out of Love

A shriek resounding
from inside.
Cold transgressions.
Aggressively clawing
at a reality.
The burning
starts to reach
closer to the core.
The final chapter,
about to unfold
into a hollow scream,
echoing in desperation
to be heard
for some resolution.
Lamenting over all
that is left.
The shuffling of feet
against the cold marble
slowly comes to a halt,
and then comes the realization
of what has now become a dream.
A rush of rejoice
washed over a heated forehead,
but once more,
the undying feeling
floats against the surface.
A reminder
of the haunting memory of hope,
the foolish thought
of a victory owned

Yasmeen Hamzeh

against a done deed.
Once more, her legs give out.
Her body, heavy with defeat.
A struggle shows
against the creases
of her tired face.
As if escaping the last fight,
her lips curve once more into a grin.
The smile cracks slowly
and falters to an emotionless line.
Her lids shut
and her head lulled back,
the final realization of what was to come
hits her ragged frame,
and she lets go of her convictions
to shrivel back
to her old ways.

An Obsession

There's lightning outside,
while on the inside,
I dream of the ways
you can light me up.
My thoughts keep drifting
to your silent smirk,
the sure sign of a winner.
I stumbled my way
into your headlights.
I had no intention
of losing
until you came into focus,
until you decided the game.
My ego keeps slipping
through my fingers,
an indication of lost time.
My bare feet long
to dance on cold ceramic tiles,
to breathe in endless plastic roses.
My luck seems to always hide from me.
One – a father,
forever bound to his little one.
The second was bound to another,
only meant for each other.
The third was my pitfall,
he was "all is fair in love and war"
until someone's heart
was ripped apart.
Now, I have nothing to lose,
because his heart

only loves the open road.
I realize
none of it really matters
as long as I can feel
the pressure from fingers.
All I need
is to admit defeat,
I had been dealt
a losing hand.
Now, I stay up late
and pray for a solution.
My heart beats on a path
my mind can't control.
Now, my feet have become tangled
in these threads.

Breaking the Dread

I only shared skin,
then expected more.
Now, all I do
is trace the rims
of empty bottles.
I grace myself in new sheets
and familiarize myself
with new expanses of skin.
My mind wouldn't follow
my footsteps.
It ran around
and chased thoughts of you instead.
I wish I could wake up
and see with new eyes.
Eyes that don't remember
the edges of your stubble,
the dimples in your back,
or the sporadic placing
of your freckles.
I wish I could wake up
with numb lips,
ones that don't long
for your fingertips.
My heart is growing thick
with the weight of you,
submerged in the need
for your comfort.
But I drank you in,
and now know

this is a losing fight.
I try to memorize the map
leading to forgetfulness.

Another shot
at feeling alive . . .
Another chance
at letting in another mistake . . .
A hopeful request
for someone with a lasting comfort,
someone that would let me
in between their ribs,
and declare it a haven.

The Collateral

Filled to the brim . . .
but there is no use
in crying over spilt milk.
The emptiness
beckons closer,
and my feet
are sinking in quicksand.
Hopes bottled up,
all of them milky-white reparations.
An empty prism
with sharp edges,
an empty shell
awaiting to be filled.
Insides hurtling in fear.
A cry to wake
what seems to have gone missing.
Soaked sponges suffocating
and filling the void.
Cowering in disgust,
a reflection – crystal-clear.
Suspended,
an empty weight.
The joke was on me.
I wished and wished,
until it all turned
empty,
until it all turned
to bile in my throat.
A loveless carcass,
chewed out to bits.
A body torn to shreds,
all by mindless longing
and empty promises.

Yasmeen Hamzeh

Longing

Each a different sea,
a sea nonetheless.
The one on your side
has a warm embrace.
Mine wraps me up
in a cold breeze
that whispers defeat.
Your beach holds sand
to thrust your feet into,
leaving a lasting impression
of your skin
against its grains.
Mine is a bed of rocks,
shooting up cold shivers
against my spine
that no longer tell lies.
Your bed is soft,
lace-wrapped,
with skin peeking through.
Mine are cold sheets,
tying me down
against an empty mattress.
One solace is firewater
that promises a softer sleep,
a diluted reality,
and memories miles away.
Long fingers,
cold skin,
and teeth remembering a taste.
Bubble-wrapped.

I wonder,
if there is a chance
to steal one last piece
of vivaciousness
to breath in and smell relief.

Fragility

It seemed, my mind
would rather be
preoccupied.
Crushed ice
to cool off the burn
on my tongue,
heady liquor
to sooth the burn
in my chest.
Tan lines
to replace the once-marked skin,
Velvet chokers
to replace the pressure,
and a new strumming
to replace the wailing.
Summer dresses
to cover my quivering
along silver rings
to cover the shaking.
Not so unexpectedly,
I glance at a familiar countenance.
So, I unravel
and everything re-wires.
I'm fighting the studying
of coincidences,
but the search is inevitable.
Old tears
stain new sheets,
old methods
replace new tricks,

and old memories
replace new concerns.

Now, it seems,
I haven't put you to bed;
Instead,
I lie in it wondering
if you're the same.

Yasmeen Hamzeh

A Wishful Hypocrite

Wanting –
a selfish state of thought.
What do I want?
I can easily
give you an answer.
I want you
to read my body,
trace my movement,
and learn
to read my lips.
I want you
to see me
and really look –
a longing for the understanding
in unassuming eyes.
I want you to learn my thoughts
without context,
to take a glimpse at a small version
of my truth.
It would scare me
to live in that moment,
fearing the end of it.
I can crack a silver lining
in half
and open up doors,
but I'll only end up
with splinters.
So, I will settle,
like one does.
I will settle
for the promise,

a promise
to skim
through my pages.
Even though I'm a story
with many layers.
But who am I
to speak
when I myself am a liar?

Yasmeen Hamzeh

Strength

Feet rooted
   deep in the ground,
      head held up high.
         Tides wash over.
        The moon
           illuminates the loss,
              but remains unwavering.

The cycle of struggle
   is never-ending.

Hope is born
   out of revelations.
      Hope tells me,
         I'm still existent,
         still alive,
            and I can make it through.

Acquaintance with strive
   was a teacher,
      teaching me
         that fighting temptations
        is a virtue,
            but hunger for survival
           is a gluttony
             I must embrace.

Just as sure
    as I'll look up
       and see the stars,
          I'll know
             I'm still here.

             My knees haven't weakened,
             and I still have miles to soar.

Rare . . .

I could barely remember
the contours
of your face,
but I memorized the way
your hands bent
and the way
your fingers curled.
Imagining them
pressed against my ribs . . .
Your name came to me
in vague shades,
but I remembered
the tone
of your voice.
I imagined
hearing you howl at night,
and whispering me secrets.
I felt the ridges
of your throaty laugh
rustle against my skin.
I pictured the vivacious color
of your eyes.
A weakness built
with all these thoughts
in my head.
They constantly multiplied
until they spilled out
onto my skin.
It only worsened the tightness
in my chest.

All because in this time and age,
I couldn't tell you
what I dearly wished
to say:
"There's a need."

Intertwining Selves

Combinations,
oxymorons,
contradictions.
All the words
that we are,
or were.
But whatever is left of us
feels like memories.
The moss, spreading
over that early morning coffee;
the dust, collecting
on those repurposed table lamps.
I have been doused in a fever,
and that drowning curiosity.
Shoulders mirroring
wooden frames,
filled on the inside
with blind faith,
and all that explodes
in the night.
Now it has fizzled out.
I can't seem
to fix the dream any longer,
or hold back the inevitable.
Only realize
how detestable . . .
So, I'm left
with constant reminders,
and drunken dreams,
spitting spiteful words
and the terrible urge
to feel the hurt.

So, now, I have been reduced down
into a bitterness
reminding me of unripe oranges
that smell so sweet
on reminiscent summer nights.

Yasmeen Hamzeh

A Dream, Not a Promise

Remember the shared daydream,
the promise we made.
You said,
we would run away;
we wouldn't stay shackled;
we would find a place
to call home.
Whether separated or not,
we would seek each other out,
meet at the usual destination –
that cozy bar in an old hotel.
Large French windows
overlooking a garden,
filled with pastel-colored flowers,
lush greens,
and the smell of fresh earth
as it rained . . .
Shadows would move freely,
illuminating the black wood
of the countertop.
A melody would play,
somehow familiar.
Sitting perched
atop slightly unstable stools,
sipping slowly,
reminiscing
on our younger dreams,
remembering mistakes,
tribulations,
and moments we shared.

Silence would grow,
cloaking us in comfort.
Breathe out a sigh of relief!
How we got away,
how we managed.
All a distant dream
and a broken promise,
as I get ready to leave.
I'll still have that dream
as I sleep.
Unfortunately,
it is a promise
no more.

Yasmeen Hamzeh

Snapshots of Loneliness

It's a slightly faded memory,
clouded by shimmering hope,
but I can still remember the motions.
The most prominent sound
was the creaking,
whether of bones
or the bed springs.
I would toss
and turn all night,
always restless.
Always a soft hissing,
when it was quiet.
But when there was sound,
it was of soft guitars strumming.
A voice that's cracked
but clearly resounds
and reminds of all the turmoil.
The view itself was confusing.
It wasn't what I had expected,
nothing too dull or dreary.
Instead,
all the colors were brighter and sharper,
except for the halo
surrounding me.
I was always in a color vacuum.
The scent was dominated
by stale cigarettes,
never a fresh cigarette smoke.
Sometimes it was the lingering aroma

of a week-old perfume,
still nestled
into the fabric of my pillow.

A reminder that time never stopped.
These are all distinctive memories,
memories of a time when I felt alone.

Yasmeen Hamzeh

The Gaping Hole

A gaping hole.
Like the feeling of loss.
Existing like spinning threads,
a part of my own body.
No answer
to how it came to be
or what completes it.
Always there
like a reminder.
A constant greed,
or an uncontrollable thirst.
A craving for hypotheticals.
A hole like the key
to perfection.
The lack of it,
like hunger.
A loss of will
and belief.
A part that grows with time.
Existing all around me,
in people whom I've never met.
I fear losing its stretching
against my ribcage.
But it goes for a trip
around my mind,
taking a walk
around my universe.
Has a small talk
with all these emotions,
and comes back

filled with wonder.
Wonder that only solidifies it
deep inside of me.
It is either destruction
or construction.
My own architect, a fuel.
What pulls me back up
from the emptiness,
before I fall from the precipice
of my own mind.

Epiphany

A perfect balance.
Appreciate it,
but do you observe the harmony
as a whole?
I see life in color,
not in black and white.
Grey, in abundance,
giving you no answer.
You look around
and realize how bad
things can get,
and sense grimness.
You must become
better at the game,
you must always run ahead.
Assert your prowess
and never give second chances.
Become brutal.
It takes a toll on you
and forces you
to forget the comfort of sleep.
When you lay awake
feeling your guts churning,
it helps you understand.
You wish to revert,
wanting to become lighter.
Both states cannot exist
without the other.
It's a need, and a condition
for their sole existence.

You have both,
sometimes in separate entities.
It's a balance
crafted with interlocking pieces.
They both belong in your arms,
needing a vacuum.
A neutral state in-between,
A perfect environment
for both to grow.
On one hand
there is destruction;
the other,
a possibility of losing.
So, I am lost in-between,
chasing redemption
that I may never grasp.

Despite Your Malignancies

You can sail the world
in your plight,
and take a look around.
Here I am,
standing at a crossroad.
My tresses,
blowing left and right.
I can feel each cold
breath slowly
descending my spine.
Along with it
come words of righteousness.
A long and ever-gazing tree,
wise with the past
and words of those who
passed.
The trunk may be sturdy,
but the roots take a hold
in old soil.
The howling wind sends it shuddering,
but my feet have learned to
dance along to the tune.
Each cut and each wound tell a story.
Maybe they're still raw,
but I won't let any feet step over their glory.
Like clay, I shape my psyche,
molding my own version of reality.
Like holding on
to a rocking boat
where each stalemate
tries to topple me over.

As a spectator,
your eyes stare on.
But you are being fooled,
and I can attest.
As I unfold,
you can sense the plot change.
Don't look at me
with unassuming eyes,
then play at holding on.
My existence
is riddled with holes,
and I chose
to let them breathe.
Wishing only for the realization
of my imperfections,
not a mending of my shape.
I can sense you
discard your own impurities
and try to pick at mine.
A perfectionist's charade.
A naive acceptance.
We paint our intertwining stories,
and in turn, forget the photographs of our reality,
a soulful mirage
of false memories.
My body is but a shell,
a porcelain covering
of my own choosing.
On the inside, the winds howl,
and I run free and wild.
Your upright silhouette
may never sift into mine.
So, don't blame
my interchanging breezes.
As I have already drawn out the line.

Yasmeen Hamzeh

A Final Comfort in Loss

The wind, tousling unkempt hair.
  Standing fully erect,
    fully aware of the surroundings.
      Ahead lay a dark and gaping forest.
      A sudden twitch,
          signaling the overcoming shivering.
            Deeper into the forest,
              lulled by a strange force.

Trudging through untamed wilderness.
  Feet never faltering,
    a path memorized
      like each bump and scar across her body.
        Breath, slowly
          breaking down
            into short gusts of air.
            Her footing,
                a quick and steady thump.

                The darkness,
        morphing and shielding her body.

            The moon's silver shines,
              bejeweling her armor.

      The swell of pride in each step,
              closer to the darkness.

This was a home,
the only true home left.

Complete at last,
not complacent.
Shedding the undying feeling
of loneliness,
the ache of helplessness.

The sudden snap of her spine,
the churning of bones.

A new metamorphosis.

Yasmeen Hamzeh

Epilogue

About the Author

Yasmeen Hamzeh is a young Jordanian writer who was raised in a family of lawyers and physicians enjoying relations with a wide base of professionals and politicians in the Jordanian society. She grew up with a learning habit of writing with style, often pursuing the ideal state of presenting her thoughts with a tone of many expressions. Having acquired such a unique talent when she was under 13 years of age, she demonstrated a capability to be a writer in her own right amongst young writers of our modern age. She wrote songs, short stories, columns, and composed lyrics of her expressions to beat the boredom of a restrictive high school environment.

Known for her social critiques, her writings became materials for political dialogue among adults. Loved by her family and friends, she innovated idealistic views about the rights of women and children, and presented her ideas with a challenge each time she took the stage, appeared on a platform, or happened to be in a gathering to speak about her state of mind and about any subject. For a professional at my age, I can describe her as "a growing boutique writer" who will after college become an attractive speech- and communications-specialist in the political and diplomatic circles.

It is not surprising what she came out to be: A fashionable writer, and I dare to say, I take pride to wait to read about her successes.

Rasim S. Abderrahim

Inner Child Press

Inner Child Press is a publishing company founded and operated by writers. Our personal publishing experiences provide us an intimate understanding of the sometimes-daunting challenges writers, new and seasoned, may face in the business of publishing and marketing their creative "Written Work".

For more information:

Inner Child Press

www.innerchildpress.com
intouch@innerchildpress.com

Inner Child Press International

building bridges of cultural understanding
www.innerchildpress.com

www.ingramcontent.com/pod-product-compliance
Lightning Source LLC
LaVergne TN
LVHW011214080426
835508LV00007B/773

9 781970 020984